GW00467930

AN APPLETREE DELUXE EDITION

BIRDS

IRELAND'S FLORA AND FAUNA

A COMPACT ILLUSTRATED GUIDE SHOWING
BIRDS IN TYPICAL POSES AS AN
AID TO IDENTIFICATION

GORDON D'ARCY

AN APPLETREE DELUXE EDITION

BIRDS

IRELAND'S FLORA AND FAUNA

A COMPACT ILLUSTRATED GUIDE SHOWING
BIRDS IN TYPICAL POSES AS AN
AID TO IDENTIFICATION

Appletree Press

First published in 2007 by
Appletree Press Ltd
The Old Potato Station
14 Howard Street South
Belfast
BT7 1AP
Tel: +44 (0) 28 90 24 30 74
Fax: +44 (0) 28 90 24 67 56
E-mail: reception@appletree.ie
Web Site: www.appletree.ie

Copyright ©Appletree Press, 1986, 1999, 2005, 2007
Text and Illustrations © Gordon D'Arcy, 1986, 1999, 2005, 2007

First published in 1986 as *Birds of Ireland* by Appletree Press Ltd

All rights reserved. Printed in China. No part of this publication may be
reproduced or transmitted in any form or by any means, electronic or
mechanical, photocopying, recording or in any information and retrieval
system without prior permission, in writing from the publisher.

A catalogue record for this book is available from the British Library.

BIRDS – IRELAND'S FLORA & FAUNA

ISBN: 978 1 84758 051 1

Desk & Marketing Editor: Jean Brown
Editor: Jim Black
Designer: Stuart Wilkinson
Production Manager: Paul McAvoy

9 8 7 6 5 4 3 2 1

AP3489

CONTENTS

Divers and grebes are related and are found in Ireland mainly on coastal waters (divers) and inland or inshore waters (grebes). They eat fish, which they catch by diving from the water surface.

This group contains four related species which spend most of their lives on or over the open sea, coming to land only to breed in colonies on coastal sites.

The Cormorant and Shag are closely related and are primarily coastal inhabitants, while the Heron is a long-necked and long-legged wading bird found in a wide variety of wetland habitats.

The swans are the most recognizable of all birds. Their very large size and white plumage make identification easy. Only the Mute Swan is a resident in Ireland; the Whooper and Bewick's are winter visitors from the Arctic.

Geese are large birds which are usually associated with wetlands. They all breed in the far north, particularly in the Arctic. Gregarious and vocal, they are characterized by their line and 'V' shape formations in flight.

CONTENTS

Dabbling ducks are also called surface-feeding ducks. They feed mainly on vegetable matter on, or close to, the surface of the water. When taking to the air they rise vertically from the water surface.

This group of ducks feeds by diving completely beneath the water surface to obtain sub-aquatic food. All have their feet far back on their bodies, an added facility to underwater swimming, and they patter the water surface when taking flight.

These birds are grouped together because of their hawk-like appearance. Only one, the Sparrowhawk, is a true hawk; three others are closely related to falcons. All, with the exception of the Cuckoo, are birds of prey.

All are 'tight-sitting' birds which use their cryptic plumage as protection against human and animal predators. They are ground birds, favouring a variety of habitats, and 'explode' into the air on being disturbed.

These birds are hen-like in appearance and behaviour. They are all reluctant fliers, preferring to run or swim away when alarmed.

CONTENTS

This group contains the four sizeable wading birds which are widespread in Ireland. All are specialist feeders, probing soft mud for different varieties of invertebrate food.

The Shanks are true waders, having long legs for life in shallow water. The Plovers, being less water dependent, may be found in drier situations. All feed by pecking or probing the soft ground.

Included here are five of Ireland's best-known small shorebirds. They are mainly found at the coast, and are mostly winter visitors from Northern Europe and the Arctic.

This group comprises Ireland's larger 'seagulls'. In reality they are commonly found inland too. They are instantly recognizable by their white bodies, grey or black wings and lazy flight. The immature birds are not so easy to identify.

Though often called 'seagulls', only the Kittiwake is essentially a 'seagull'; the others are also frequent inland. All are readily identifiable in adult plumage but are perhaps more difficult to recognize in immature plumage.

CONTENTS

The terns are close relations of the gulls but are more lightly built, with a streamlined and graceful appearance. They are all summer visitors to Ireland, wintering mainly in the south Atlantic.

This group comprises the auks. The feet of these seabirds are placed so far back that they have an upright, penguin-like appearance on the ground. Auks breed in vast 'bird cities' on cliffs around the coasts. In winter they vacate their coastal breeding grounds for the open sea.

Pigeons and doves belong to the same family. All are ground feeders which are capable of quick, vertical take-off. They are noted for their tender courtship behaviour and soft cooing calls.

These birds are closely related and have in common the fact that they live mainly on the ground and are adapted to running rather than hopping. In addition, they feed mainly on insects which are caught on or near the ground.

These birds are adapted to life in the air, having a streamlined shape, swept-back wings and forked tail. All are long-distance migrants which winter in Africa.

Contents

These four species have in common their small size, predominantly brownish plumage and diet, which consists of insects.

The thrushes are instantly recognizable by their brownish plumage and speckled underparts. The Song Thrush and Mistle Thrush are well-known garden birds found in Ireland all year round. The Redwing and Fieldfare are winter visitors from northern Europe.

The Blackbird and Starling are very familiar garden birds, many of which live and breed in close proximity to man. The Dipper and Kingfisher are generally associated with streams and rivers and usually afford only fleeting glimpses.

These birds are small but clearly marked and coloured. They are not secretive and perch in obvious places, usually near the ground.

This group comprises very small insect-eaters that move about secretively in foliage and are normally difficult to observe as a result.

Contents

This is a group of small birds which are well known for their nimble feeding behaviour and their attractive looks. Although woodland species initially, they have become garden birds as well, and coexist comfortably with man.

The four crows described - Magpie, Jackdaw, Rook, Hooded Crow - are well known as resourceful and intelligent birds. Unfortunately this has gained them a bad reputation in some circumstances.

The Raven, Jay and Chough tend to shun man and inhabit areas where they can live undisturbed. All have characteristic calls by which they may be identified even without being seen.

This group contains five attractive seed-eating birds. They are primarily woodland or open country species but may be found in gardens too. All have distinctive calls by which they may be identified.

These are mainly finches or their relatives. Their bills are stout and adapted for feeding on seeds. They are mainly resident in Ireland, and occupy a variety of habitats.

INTRODUCTION

ABOUT THIS BOOK

A total of 123 birds has been covered in this book. These are the birds that could be considered to be 'widespread' in Ireland. This does not mean that they are abundant or common, as this depends on the density of distribution. One or two birds have been omitted which could be considered as fairly widespread and one or two have been included which are not yet widespread but look like becoming so.

The birds in the book have been grouped together, generally in threes, fours or fives, under a particular heading. This may be because they are of the same family, are related to one another, or simply have something in common. In some the connection may seem a little contrived but it has been necessary, for the sake of compactness, to group them as such.

The text for each of the birds is given with the colour illustration of the bird. Each is given an English, Scientific and Irish name in that order. The description of each species is brief, concentrating on the important features for identification. Everyday phrases (such as 'rust-coloured' or 'dumpy-looking') are used instead of more formal terminology and the size of the birds, where mentioned, is given as either small, medium or large (small means up to Blackbird size; medium, up to Woodpigeon size; large, greater than this).

The illustrations show the birds in typical poses. Some flight views are shown also where these are useful for identification. Where there is a significant difference in plumage between male and female, from summer to winter or where the young bird may cause difficulties, these are shown too.

BIRDWATCHING

Birdwatching is good fun. It's a leisure activity for all the family - age doesn't matter. You don't need expensive equipment, your God-given faculties will do! After a while it may be necessary to buy a pair of binoculars but good binoculars can now be obtained quite cheaply. The type to look for are 8 x 40 or equivalent, and there are many good makes.

You can birdwatch anywhere. The back garden, the local wood, the estuary, the coast and the mountains all support birds. It may be possible to see a dozen different kinds in the garden but you may see fifty at an estuary or on the coast.

Take time to identify the different kinds (species) and watch how they live. Birds have feeding grounds, roosting grounds and breeding areas and many also migrate to warmer countries for the winter. If you write down the ones you see in summer and compare those seen in winter it becomes obvious that some of our birds leave in winter but others come here from other countries too.

It adds to the enjoyment of a country walk or a picnic if you take notice of the birds that you see on the way. It's a good idea to take notes and make sketches as well, as this helps to tune the senses. Birdwatching teaches you to look and listen and, perhaps more importantly, to be *aware* of your surroundings. It is by being aware that you can learn to understand nature and how we, as people, relate to it.

So there's more to birdwatching than meets the eye!

ABBREVIATIONS

ad: adult
imm: immature
f: female
juv: juvenile
m: male
sum: summer plumage
win: winter plumage

Note: 'immature' refers to *any* sub-adult bird - that is, any bird which has not yet reached maturity and acquired the plumage of the adult bird. 'Juvenile' refers to the first-year state only, during which the chick or young bird wears plumage which it will lose at its first moult.

DIVER-TYPE BIRDS

Red-throated Diver
Gavia stellata
Lóma rua

sum.   win.

The Red-throated Diver breeds mainly in northern Europe and has a fine plumage with brick-red throat at this time. As a widespread winter visitor to inshore coastal waters it is usually seen in Ireland in its rather drab winter plumage – grey, finely speckled white above; white below and on the face. Though distinctly smaller than the Great-northern Diver, this species is nevertheless quite large. It has a recognizable profile when sitting on the water, with a slightly up-tilted bill position.

Great-northern Diver
Gavia immer
Lóma mór

sum.

win.

The Great-northern Diver is, as the name suggests, mainly an Arctic breeder. It occurs as a widespread winter visitor to inshore coastal waters. Only in breeding plumage does it have the fine black-and-white plumage with barred neck band and back patches. In winter plumage, when it is most common in Ireland, it is, like the Red-throated Diver, quite drab, dark grey above and whitish below and on the face. The head and bill are large and rather angular looking and noticeable from even long range.

Great-crested Grebe
Podiceps cristatus
Foitheach mór

sum.

win.

The Great-crested Grebe both breeds and winters in Ireland. The breeding habitat is usually in a lake and the majority spend the winter on estuaries or other inshore waters at the coast. A medium-sized bird with a long neck, this grebe has a strikingly beautiful summer plumage. Both male and female have unusual and elaborate head plumage used in nuptial display. In winter the plumage is dark grey above, white below, on the front of the neck, face and above the eye – a "ghostly" looking bird. In the rather laboured flight the wings show clear white patches.

Little Grebe
Tachybaptus ruficollis
Spáigaire tonn

win.

sum.

The Little Grebe, or Dabchick, is very small and dumpy in shape. It is brownish overall with rust-coloured cheeks in summer and yellow bill-gape. In winter it is greyer and paler. It is a widespread breeder in ponds and small lakes with aquatic vegetation. The Little Grebe is hyperactive, diving constantly from the water surface for food. Both this and the Great-crested Grebe have the endearing habit of carrying their chicks "piggy-back" fashion on the water near the nest. Dabchicks make an unusual "whinnying" sound at the breeding site.

OCEAN-GOING BIRDS

Fulmar
Fulmarus glacialis
Fulmaire

The Fulmar is much more "seagull-like"
than the others in this group and is often
mistaken for one. The wings are grey as in
the gulls but so is the back and tail (white in
the gulls). The thick yellow bill and deep-
set, dark eyes in the heavy white head
look different from those of the gulls.
The shearing and stiff-winged flight
is more like that of the shearwaters
than the gulls. The nest is usually
on a sea cliff and colonies are found
all around the Irish coast in suitable
habitats.

Gannet
Sula bassana
Gainéad

One of Ireland's most obvious sea
birds; larger than the biggest gulls,
with brilliant white plumage and
black wing tips. Only the adult is
white – the juvenile is dark grey
with fine white speckling, and
gets progressively whiter until
full plumage in its third year.
Gannets may be seen fishing
anywhere around Irish coasts
but there are only a few
breeding colonies, on islands
on the south and west
coasts.

ad.

juv.

Manx Shearwater
Puffinus puffinus
Cánóg dhubh

The Manx Shearwater is much smaller
than the Gannet, with a striking pattern
of black above and white below. It has
a most recognizable flight. Lines of
shearwaters glide close to the waves,
showing at one minute black uppersides
and at the next, white undersides. They nest
in colonies in holes in the ground on cliff
tops or similar locations and approach
the nests under cover of darkness.
As birds of the open sea, Manx
Shearwaters are unusual inshore
during the winter.

Storm Petrel
Hydrobates pelagicus
Guairdeall

The Storm Petrel is not often seen in Ireland,
though countless thousands of them breed in
nest-hole colonies in locations along the western
seaboard. As with the Manx Shearwater, it comes
to the nest at night-time only. It is a tiny bird
(about the size of a House Martin) which, having
a white rump, is sometimes mistaken for a petrel.
The plumage is sooty black relieved only by the
noticeable white rump. During and after storms it
may sometimes be seen on inshore coastal waters.

LONG-NECKED BIRDS

Cormorant
Phalacrocorax carbo
Broigheall

The Cormorant is a large, long-necked diving bird, often incorrectly called a "diver". It feeds by plunging from the water surface and catching fish, which it swallows on the surface. It is well known for its habit of stretching out it wings to dry while standing at its roost. The plumage is glossy black and in summer the adult has white patches on the face and flanks. The immature birds are much browner than the adults and are pale on the entire underparts. Cormorants nest in colonies on rocky coastal islands and headlands and also in trees alongside some inland lakes.

Shag
Phalacrocorax aristotelis
Seaga

he Shag is a smaller version of the Cormorant but is strictly coastal. In habits
d general behaviour it resembles the larger bird. Its plumage is blackish but has
distinctly greenish sheen and lacks the white patches on face and flanks. The
eeding bird sports a tufted crest and bright yellow bill-gape. The immature bird
like the immature cormorant, pale on the face and the underparts and dark
own on the upperparts. Shags nest colonially, often amongst other seabirds on
cky islets and cliffs.

Grey Heron
Ardea cinerea
Corr riasc

The Grey Heron needs little description, being so well known as to be a favourite subject of Irish folklore. Its singular appearance, both on the ground and in the air, has long drawn the attention of even the least observant of people. It is one of Ireland's largest birds, with a slow, ponderous flight. The legs protrude beyond the tail of the flying Heron but the long neck is tucked back, giving a "blunt-fronted" look. The plumage is basically grey above and white below but there is a distinctive black streak above and behind the eye extending to a long plume. Long plumes are found also on the neck, breast and back of the adult. The young bird is duller and less strikingly marked than the adult. Herons nest in colonies in the tops of high trees, and sometimes nearer the ground on islands in lakes.

SWANS

Mute Swan
Cygnus olor
Eala bhalbh

ad.

imm.

The Mute Swan needs little description, its beauty having captivated man for centuries. The puffed-out back feathers and gracefully curved neck are well-known features of this bird. The bill is orange and has a black knob at the base. In flight the wings make a tuneful "wheezing" sound but, as its name suggests, it is more or less vocally silent. The nest is a massive affair, often in an inaccessible spot in a reedbed or along a river. The cygnets are greyish and have an endearing appearance. The adults are less "innocent", with aggressive tendencies, sometimes feeding on young birds as well as their more staple diet of aquatic plants.

Whooper Swan
Cygnus cygnus
Eala ghlórach

ad.

imm.

The Whooper Swan is as large as the Mute Swan but has a less graceful form. A distant flock can look stiff-necked and somewhat angular compared with Mutes. Flocks of Whoopers make, however, the most tuneful sounds, adding atmosphere to stark winter wetlands. The bill is bright yellow with a black tip and the head and bill combined have a wedge-shaped appearance. The young are greyish with pinkish, black-tipped bills. Whooper Swans often feed on riverside callows and other low-lying ground near wetlands, and can look like grazing sheep from a distance. They are fairly widespread visitors to Ireland's larger inland wetlands.

Bewick's Swan
Cygnus columbianus
Eala Bhewick

ad.

imm.

The Bewick's Swan is like a smaller version of the Whooper Swan. Like the larger bird, the bill is yellow and black but there is less yellow than black. The head shape too is more rounded and less wedge-shaped than that of the Whooper Swan. The young are dull grey with pinkish, dark-tipped bills. The calls of the Bewick's Swan are similar to those of the Whooper but less musical. Wild swans often feed in fields and when Bewicks are intermixed with Whoopers they may be difficult to distinguish. Less widespread than the Whoopers, Bewicks are nonetheless regular winter visitors to many of the larger Irish wetlands.

GEESE

White-fronted Goose (top right)
Anser albifrons
Gé bháneadanach

The Greenland White-fronted Goose is smaller than the Greylag. It is much browner and darker and gets its name from the small white patch on the forehead (though this is absent in the young birds). The best distinguishing features from a distance are the heavy black blotches on the under parts of the adult. In flight it shows less grey on the wings than does the Greylag and the call is a more high pitched yelping. The White-fronted Goose is now mainly confined to the Wexford Wildfowl Reserve, though scattered flocks overwinter elsewhere.

Greylag Goose (middle right)
Anser anser
Gé glas

The largest of the geese is the Greylag, so called because of the large, pale grey patches on the wings. The overall colour is grey-brown, with a large white area beneath the tail and a smaller one on the rump visible in flight. The large orange bill and pink legs are good identification features and are visible from a long way off. When disturbed or in flight, the Greylag makes loud confused honking calls and sounds very like the farmyard goose. The favoured habitats are extensive callows and reclaimed scrubland.

Barnacle Goose (bottom right)
Branta leucopsis
Gé ghiiirainn

Almost all of Ireland's wintering Barnacle Geese are found in islands on the west and north coasts, to which they migrate from Arctic Greenland each year. The most striking of geese to be seen in Ireland, its grey and black-and-white patterns of plumage make identification straightforward. In flight, extensive grey patches show on the wings and the flock calls with a noisy yelping. The main habitat is on low, grassy islands but flocks also commute to coastal fields on the mainland.

Brent Goose
Branta bernicla
Cadhan

The Brent Goose is the smallest of Ireland's geese, being not much larger than a Mallard Duck. The pale-bellied form (the form occurring in Ireland) is greyish on the belly and flanks. Brent Geese have small white markings on the sides of the neck and the bill is very small. The young have pale edges to some of the feathers on the back. Flocks of Brents call with a low "gurgling" noise both on the ground and in the air. They feed on eel grass and other marine plants on coastal mudflats, their primary habitat.

DABBLING DUCKS

Shelduck
Tadorna tadorna
Seil-lacha

The Shelduck is Ireland's largest duck – the size of a small goose. It is surprisingly common and widespread as a winter visitor to muddy estuaries and inlets. It is also a widespread breeder in Ireland. The Shelduck is strikingly beautiful, with its black-and-white plumage, orange breast band, under-tail patch and dark green head. The sexes are alike, though the male is larger and has a conspicuous knob on top of the bright red bill.

Wigeon
Anas penelope
Rualacha

The Wigeon is an abundant winter visitor from northern Europe to Ireland. Flocks are to be found in grassy places alongside lakes, estuaries and some large rivers. On the ground, Wigeon can be quite inconspicuous despite their fine plumage but in the air they are very obvious. The males have large white wing patches and they call continuously with a far-carrying whistle "whee-oo". The female is dull and brownish.

Teal
Anas crecca
Praslacha ghlaseiteach

f.   m.

The Teal is Ireland's smallest duck, being little bigger than a Moorhen. In winter it is more widespread and abundant than it appears. The drake is a beautiful but subtly marked bird with rust-coloured and shiny green head, spotted breast and finely marked grey body. As with most other ducks, the female is dull and brownish. Teal call from the water with a curious ringing note when anxious. Some Teal stay and breed in Irish wetlands but they are not common breeders.

Mallard
Anas platyrhynchos
Mallard

The Mallard is the common "wild duck" of the ponds and ditches. A large duck, the male is a fine bird with greyish body, bright orange legs, yellowish bill and curly black feathers above the tail. The female is dowdy brown with a pale eyestripe. Both sexes have a blue-green patch on the wing, edged on both sides with white. The Mallard nests in a wide variety of situations near water.

Shoveler
Anas clypeata
Spadalghob

The Shoveler is roughly the same size as the Wigeon but very different in appearance. The drake is a striking bird, showing a lot of white but with a blackish head, huge bill and obvious rust-coloured sides. The female is dull brownish. Both male and female have conspicuous light blue wing patches, obvious in flight. The Shoveler is a widespread but thinly distributed winter visitor, mainly to freshwater wetlands but also to some estuaries. Very few breed in Ireland.

DIVING DUCKS

Pochard
Aythya ferina
Poiseard

f.   m.

The Pochard is quite widespread as a winter visitor to Irish lakes – it is even
abundant in some places. Unlike the Tufted Duck, it only rarely breeds in Ireland
The male Pochard is greyish with black breast and rear end. The head is deep
rust-coloured. The female is much duller. In flight, both sexes show pale grey
wing bars and the flight is rapid and direct like that of the Tufted Duck, to which
it is similar in size and shape.

Tufted Duck
Aythya fuligula
Lacha bhadánach

f.   m.

The Tufted Duck is a widespread and, in some places, abundant winter visitor. Although smallish in size, the pied plumage of the males makes them easily recognizable from a distance. Only the male has the tuft on the back of the head; the female is dull chocolate brown. In flight, a clear white bar shows on the wings of both sexes. Tufted Ducks stay to nest on islets on a few of Ireland's larger lakes.

Eider
Somateria mollissima
Éadar lacha

Ireland's largest diving duck, the Eider is exclusively coastal, favouring rock
areas where it can dive for its favourite foods. The male is unmistakable –
predominantly white sea-duck with a black patch on the sides and other le
noticeable black and coloured marks. The female is heavily barred and brownis
Both sexes have a most striking wedge-shaped bill and head. Eiders make stran
human-sounding notes when they are displaying.

Goldeneye
Bucephala clangula
Orshúileach

The Goldeneye is a widespread but thinly distributed winter visitor from northern Europe. The plumage of the male is striking, with predominantly white body and contrasting glossy black head, with a white spot near the base of the bill. The female is dull brownish with a pale neck band. In flight, the Goldeneye is particularly noticeable due to the large white wing patches and the curious ringing noise made by the wings.

Red-breasted Merganser
Mergus serrator
Síolta rua

f.   m.

The Red-breasted Merganser is a widespread resident in Irish inshore coasta
waters and larger lakes. Mergansers have particularly streamlined bodies, enablin
swift movement underwater. The male is beautifully marked black, white an
greyish. The female is greyish brown with red-brown head. Both sexes have ver
thin red bills. In the air Mergansers fly swiftly and show large white wing patche
rather like those of the Goldeneye.

HAWK-LIKE BIRDS

Sparrowhawk
Accipiter nisus
Spioróg

The Sparrowhawk is Ireland's most widespread bird of prey. It hunts by flying fast and low and by ambushing its prey. The wings are short and rounded for quick acceleration and to facilitate hunting in confined areas. The tail is noticeably long. The male Sparrowhawk is blue-grey above, barred reddish below; the female is grey-brown above and barred dark below.

Kestrel
Falco tinnunculus
Pocaire gaoithe

The Kestrel is Ireland's most common and widespread falcon, hunting mainly in open country. It hovers as if suspended by an invisible thread, eyes fixed on the ground below, and swoops down to capture its prey. The male is light red-brown on the back, heavily spotted with black; the head and tail are light blue-grey. The underparts are creamy, spotted with black. The female is larger and duller coloured and is barred rather than spotted.

Peregrine
Falco peregrinus
Fabhcín gorm

This is Ireland's largest and most dynamic falcon. The main prey in the wild are medium-sized birds like pigeons. The Peregrine is heavily built but retains the falcon flight profile. The male is slate-grey above, whitish barred with black below. There are very noticeable black facial marks contrasting with the white cheeks. The larger female is similar but the young bird is browner above and streaked, not barred, below.

Merlin
Falco columbarius
Meirliún

The Merlin is Ireland's smallest falcon but is a highly mobile and effective hunter, being usually found in wild moorland. In winter it often hunts in coastal habitats. The male Merlin is only the size of a Blackbird. It is slate-grey above, whitish streaked reddish below. The female and immature birds are brownish above, whitish streaked dark below. The flight profile is like that of a scaled-down Peregrine.

Cuckoo
Cuculus canorus
Cuach

The Cuckoo is a rather mysterious bird, being much more often heard than seen. It is a summer visitor from winter quarters in Africa. Cuckoos like open country, where they search for the nests of potential foster parents for their offspring. The adult Cuckoo is grey above, white barred with black below and has a long barred tail. The young are rich brown and heavily barred all over. Cuckoos look particularly hawk-like in flight.

GAME BIRDS

Pheasant
Phasianus colchicus
Piasún

f.   m.

The Pheasant is an introduced bird which has been in Ireland for centuries. The largest of Ireland's game birds, it is so familiar as to require little description. The cinnamon-coloured plumage of the male is heavily spotted with black and the extraordinarily long tail is barred along its length. The female is duller but is also heavily barred and lacks the long tail of the male.

Red Grouse
Lagopus lagopus
Cearc fhraoigh

f.   m.

The Red Grouse is a bird of moorland and bog, where its staple foods, the shoots and berries of heathers and associated plants, are found. The Irish Red Grouse is a medium-sized but very dumpy bird. The male is heavily mottled red-brown, causing it to blend into its heathery surroundings. A bright red wattle is noticeable over the eye. The female is overall paler. On being flushed, grouse appear very dark except for whitish underwing patches. They call with human-sounding notes often described as sounding like the words "go-back".

Snipe
Gallinago gallinago
Naoscach

The Snipe is similar to the Woodcock but smaller and camouflaged more for hiding in marshy vegetation than on the woodland floor. The rich brownish plumage is broken up with straw-like streaks. The very long bill is used for probing in soft mud for food. When the marshes are frozen in cold weather, Snipe seek food at springs or even on dry, rough ground. The Snipe's name is descriptive of its sharp call – a typical wetland sound.

Woodcock
Scolopax rusticola
Creabhar

Although the Woodcock breeds in Ireland it is more widespread as a winter visitor. It is not easy to get a good look at this bird for it either sits perfectly camouflaged on the ground amongst dead vegetation or else flies away rapidly through the trees. It is medium-sized and very dumpy in shape with broad, rounded wings and short tail. The bill is very long and straight – ideal for probing in soft ground for food. The rust-coloured plumage is heavily barred and the sexes are alike. Breeding Woodcocks are territorial and the male flies around his "beat" at dusk.

GROUND AND WATER 'HENS'

Corncrake
Crex crex
Traonach

The Corncrake is sadly decreasing throughout western Europe due to a number of factors. It is now much less widespread than formerly but still breeds in parts of the west of Ireland. It is a medium-sized, brownish bird with rust-coloured wing patches and barred flanks. Corncrakes are rarely seen and identification using the call is reliable. This is a raucous shout – "aic-aic" – uttered from the cover of a rough meadow or similar location.

Water Rail
Rallus aquaticus
Rallóg uisce

The Water Rail is another secretive bird, much more often heard than seen. The calls are strange and varied, the most familiar being a piglet-like squealing. It is slightly smaller and slimmer than the Corncrake and more attractively marked. The upper parts are red-brown, streaked darker; the face and underparts are slate-grey and there is black-and-white barring on the flanks. In flight the reddish pink legs often dangle. The bill is also reddish and is long and slightly downcurved. Although resident in Ireland, Water Rails also turn up at coastal islands on migration.

46

Moorhen
Gallinula chloropus
Cearc uisce

The Moorhen, known also as the "Waterhen", is a common and widespread resident, inhabiting wetland locations throughout Ireland. It is a medium-sized, sooty bird with long greenish legs and bright red, yellow-tipped bill. There is white marking along the edges of the flanks and a clear white patch beneath the tail. This is jerked up and down and the head is nodded as it walks or swims. The calls are a series of shrill squawks, mostly uttered from cover.

Coot
Fulica atra
Cearc cheannann

The Coot favours permanent wetlands like larger ponds and lakes. It is larger than the Moorhen, with a bulkier body, and, like the Moorhen, nods its head whilst swimming. Overall blackish in colour, it has a distinctive white bill and shield on the forehead. Coots dive from the water surface for underwater food. On being disturbed they scuttle along the surface of the water in a half-hearted attempt at flight. The Coot calls its own name – a resonant "coot" – revealing its presence even from the midst of reeds.

LARGER WADERS

Curlew
Numenius arquata
Crotach

The largest of the waders is the Curlew – a well-known Irish bird which not only arrives in winter hordes but also breeds in suitable Irish localities. It is a leggy, light brown bird, heavily streaked and flecked and with a downcurved bill 2.5 cm (6 inches) long, with which it probes for food. In flight, the rump and finely barred tail are white. The wild call from which the name is derived is a familiar sound of wetland pasture and bog, the Curlew's breeding habitats. Curlews feed on agricultural land as well as mudflats.

Bar-tailed Godwit
Limosa lapponica
Guilbneach striocearrach

win.

The Bar-tailed Godwit is like the Curlew in many respects. It too is a bird of the open mudflats (though not exclusively so) where it probes for invertebrate food using its long, slightly upturned bill. In winter plumage it resembles the Curlew both on the ground and in flight but it is much less vocal than the larger bird. A widespread winter visitor to Ireland from the Arctic, it is unusual to see it in its brick-red summer plumage in this country.

Black-tailed Godwit
Limosa limosa
Guilbneach earrdhubh

win.

The Black-tailed Godwit is also a winter visitor and passage migrant to Ireland from breeding grounds in Continental Europe. It is similar to the Bar-tailed Godwit on the ground, though the bill and legs are slightly longer, but in flight it has a striking white wing bar and rump and, as the name implies, a black tail. This godwit is not restricted to coastal habitats, but occurs inland in marshy habitats also. In summer plumage (scarce in Ireland) the Black-tailed Godwit is like the Bar-tailed, reddish in colour, though with black bars on the flanks.

Oystercatcher
Haematopus ostralegus
Roilleach

The Oystercatcher is a large black-and-white shore bird. It is striking both on the ground and in the air. A broad white bar shows on the wings in flight. In all plumages the bill is bright orange and very noticeable. The legs are pink. The end of the thick bill is quite blunt and used to hammer open the shellfish on which the Oystercatcher feeds. The call is a clear pipe, a familiar sound of the shoreline The masses of Oystercatchers on Irish shores in winter are mainly visitors from elsewhere in Europe, though many breed in Ireland also.

MEDIUM-SIZED WADERS

Redshank
Tringa totanus
Cosdeargán

The Redshank is one of Ireland's commonest and most widespread shorebirds. The majority are winter visitors or migrants from elsewhere in Northern Europe, though they breed in Ireland as well. On the ground the Redshank is a nondescript brownish bird, paler on the underparts but with long, bright orange-red legs. In flight the wings show clear white trailing edges – a very noticeable fieldmark. The call is a clear whistle, "tiu-oo-oo".

Greenshank
Tringa nebularia
Ladhrán glas

The Greenshank is slightly larger than the Redshank, with a slightly upturned, not straight, bill. The long legs are grey-green, not orange-red. The overall plumage is greyer, especially in winter plumage. In flight the Greenshank lacks the pale wing edges of the Redshank, and a long white wedge shows on the rump. The flight call is a clear whistle, "tu-tu-tu", quite different from the Redshank's. It is a widespread though thinly distributed migrant and winter visitor.

Lapwing
Vanellus vanellus
Pilibín

The Lapwing is one of Ireland's most familiar waders. The majority are winter visitors, but many also breed in Ireland. The Lapwing looks black and white from a distance but in fact the upperparts have a greenish gloss, visible from close range. A remarkable upward-pointing plume is visible on the head, though this is absent in the young birds. In the air the wings are noticeably rounded and the flight is buoyant. The call is thin and nasal.

Golden Plover
Pluvialis apricaria
Feadóg bhuí

sum.   win.

The Golden Plover is another well-known winter visitor to Ireland. It is also a scarce breeding bird. Two races occur here – Northern and Southern. The Southern race is distinguished from the Northern race by incomplete blackish underparts and face. In winter the races are identical – golden brown above and on the breast, paler below. The call is a rather sad-sounding note.

Grey Plover
Pluvialis squatarola
Feadóg ghlas

win.   sum.

The Grey Plover does not breed in Ireland, being a winter visitor from northern Europe to Irish coastal mudflats. In summer it is similar to the Northern Golden Plover but with silver, not gold-flecked, upperparts. In winter it looks like a silvery counterpart of the Golden Plover, except in flight, when the clear white rump and wing bar and unusual black "armpits" can be seen. The call note recalls that of the Golden Plover but is somewhat extended.

SMALLER WADERS

Turnstone
Arenaria interpres
Piardálaí trá

win.

sum.

The Turnstone is a well-known winter visitor from the Arctic to rocky and seaweedy shores. In winter the dull, mottled greys and browns of the plumage merge with the background and Turnstones can be difficult to see well. In summer plumage they are more conspicuous. In flight they are conspicuous in all plumages. The wing pattern is composed of clear black-and-white bars. The flight call is a series of stuttered notes quite unlike any of the other smaller waders.

Knot
Calidris canutus
Cnota

win.

The Knot is another Arctic species which comes to Ireland for the winter months. It occurs mainly on coastal mudflats. At the regular resorts Knots are very gregarious, forming flocks that can be difficult to locate against a background of grey mud. Close up, the Knot can be seen to be a dull grey bird, paler on the underparts. Even in flight it shows no clear-cut identification features. In summer plumage (which is unusual in Ireland) it is transformed into a predominantly brick-red wader.

Dunlin
Calidris alpina
Breacóg

win.

sum.

The sparrow-sized Dunlin is an abundant and widespread migrant and winter
visitor and breeds in a few places. In winter plumage it is greyish above,
whitish below and the bill and legs are black. The bill is quite long and slightly
downcurved. The flight pattern has a dark band running up the tail and rump
and a thin white wing bar. In summer plumage it is rust-brown above and there
is a black belly patch. The call is a thin, buzzing trill.

Sanderling
Calidris alba
Luathrán

In winter plumage the Sanderling is an even paler bird than the Dunlin – silvery grey above, white below and on the head. In flight the pattern is also Dunlin-like but more striking. The flight call is a clear "whit-whit", noticeably different from the Dunlin's. In summer plumage the Sanderling is rich brown on the upperparts and on the breast and clear white on most of the underparts. They are widespread migrants and winter visitors.

Ringed Plover
Charadrius hiaticula
Feadóg chladaigh

The Ringed Plover has an unmistakable plumage pattern. The upperparts are brown, the underparts white, but there is a neat black breast band and black facial markings. The legs and bill are orange, the latter with a black tip. In flight it has a wing pattern similar to that of the Dunlin. The flight call is a more tuneful "prrip". Ringed Plovers are widespread migrants and winter visitors and breed in Ireland as well.

LARGER GULLS

Herring Gull
Larus argentatus
Faoileán scadán

ad.   imm.

The Herring Gull is perhaps Ireland's commonest and most widespread gull, being found almost anywhere where food is available. The majority of nesting colonies are on coastal cliffs and islands but it has taken to nesting on city buildings and elsewhere. The plumage of the adult is mainly white with grey wings and back. The wing tips are black with white spots. The legs are pink; the bill is yellow with a red spot on the lower half. Juvenile Herring Gulls are grey-brown, heavily mottled darker and the bill is all dark. The immature birds have paler plumage and dark-tipped bills. Herring Gulls call with a well-known high-pitched yelping.

Great Black-backed Gull
Larus marinus
Droimneach mór

ad.   imm.

The Great Black-backed Gull is easily recognized by its white body, black back and wings and large size. Like the Herring Gull, the legs are pink and the bill, which is larger and more vicious-looking than that of the Herring Gull, is also yellow with a red spot on the lower half. The young bird follows the same plumage development of the other gulls but is recognizable in any plumage by its large size, heavy build and massive bill. Great Black-backs nest in coastal localities often amongst colonies of other gulls. The call of the Great Black-backed Gull is deeper than that of the Herring or Lesser Black-backed Gulls.

Lesser Black-backed Gull
Larus fuscus
Droimneach beag

ad.   imm.

The Lesser Black-backed Gull is identical to the Herring Gull in size and shape but has dusky grey wings and back (intermediate in shade between the Herring Gull and the Great Black-backed Gull). The legs of this species are yellow, not pink as in the other large gulls. It is difficult to distinguish between young Lesser Black-backs and young Herring Gulls, especially in the juvenile plumage. Lesser Black-backs are largely migratory and are not usually found in Ireland in winter. The colonies that nest here do so mainly on islets on the larger lakes and, though there are many colonies, it is nowhere particularly numerous.

SMALLER GULLS

Black-headed Gull
Larus ridibundus
Faoileán ceanndhubh

juv.

sum.

win.

The Black-headed Gull in fact has a dark brown head – and this only in summer plumage. In winter plumage only a blackish spot remains, behind the eye. The best identification feature, however, is the white front to the wings which is an obvious feature in all plumages. Even the young, which are mottled brown above and have a black tip to the tail, show the white forewing. The bill and legs of the adult are red; those of the immature bird are yellowish, the bill having a black tip. The calls are unpleasant, raucous notes and are somewhat like those of the terns. The colony is usually located on a low islet or marshy place and the nests are placed very close together.

Common Gull
Larus canus
Faoileán bán

juv.

The Common Gull is badly named, for it is by no means Ireland's commonest gull. It nests in colonies on some inland lakes. In appearance it resembles a smaller version of the Herring Gull, having white body, grey back and wings with black tips. The wing tips are noticeably marked with white and the legs and bill are greyish green, not pink and yellow as in the larger bird. The immature bird is mottled grey-brown above and the tail has a thick black terminal band. In flight the front of the immature bird's wings are noticeably darker than the rear. The call is a pleasant mewing.

Kittiwake
Rissa tridactyla
Saidhbhéar

juv.

The Kittiwake could be described as a coastal counterpart of the Common Gull, being similar in size and general shape. The back and wings are grey, the latter with black "dipped-in ink" tips. The bill is dull yellow and the legs are black. There are clear black markings on the upperparts of the immature bird: on the back of the neck, on the tip of the tail and diagonally across the wings. Kittiwake nest in colonies on sea cliffs and stacks all around Irish coasts, and often associate with other seabirds like Auks and Fulmars. The name is derived from the call at the nesting site, which is unmistakably "kittiwake".

TERNS

Common Tern
Sterna hirundo
Geabhróg

The Common Tern is grey on the back and wings and white over the remainder of the plumage except for a striking black cap on the head. The bill and short legs are red, the former with a black tip. The call is usually uttered on the wing and is a harsh "k-reeagh". The young birds are mottled with black and brown on the upperparts, have a partial black cap on the head and lack the deeply forked tail of the adults. Common Terns nest in colonies along coastal sandspits and coastal or lake islets.

Arctic Tern
Sterna paradisaea
Geabhróg artach

The Arctic Tern resembles the Common Tern in many ways. The differences are subtle, the most obvious being a greyish tinge on the underparts, highlighting the white cheeks; the deeper red bill lacking the black tip; the shorter red legs. Despite these differences, identification is difficult, especially when they are breeding together in large mixed colonies. The young are almost identical to young Common Terns.

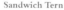

Sandwich Tern
Sterna sandvicensis
Geabhróg dhúscothach

The Sandwich Tern is the largest of Ireland's terns and is more gull-like than the others. In bulk it is equivalent to the smaller gulls. The tail is less noticeably forked than either the Common or the Arctic Terns. From a distance it looks overall whitish, the back and wings being the palest grey. The black cap on the head is shaggy at the rear. The bill is long, black and yellow-tipped and the short legs are also black. The young are, as in the other terns, mottled on the upperparts. The call is a loud, grating "kro-ick".

Little Tern
Sterna albifrons
Geabhróg bhídeach

The Little Tern is much smaller than the others described. The main features are a white forehead in summer plumage, short yellow legs and black-tipped bill and a thin rasping call. The tail is only slightly forked and the flight is noticeably light and dainty. The young have striking diagonal wing markings but are smaller than other species for which they might be mistaken. The nesting colonies are restricted to a small number of beaches on Irish coasts.

PENGUIN-LIKE BIRDS

Guillemot
Uria aalge
Foracha

win.

sum.

The Guillemot is the largest of this group and is found in many colonies around Irish coasts. The noise of these colonies has to be heard to be believed – the cumulative effect sounds like weird gargling. The bird itself is warm brown on the upperparts, head and neck, white below and on the edge of the wings. The bill is black and dagger-shaped, the legs blackish also. In winter the Guillemot becomes duller on the upperparts and the face turns whitish.

Razorbill
Alca torda
Crosán

win.   sum.

The Razorbill is similar to the Guillemot in size and shape but sits less upright. Razorbills usually breed in association with Guillemots on the sea cliffs. They are black rather than dark brown on the upperparts, head and neck and there are intricate fine white lines on the bill, which is deeper and less dagger-shaped than that of the Guillemot. In winter plumage they become whitish on the face like the Guillemot.

Black Guillemot
Cepphus grylle
Foracha dhubh

win.   sum.

The Black Guillemot is smaller and less gregarious than the larger bird. It favours piers, harbours and rocky locations close to the edge of the sea. In summer plumage the Black Guillemot is indeed black but with large white wing patches. The legs and feet are strikingly red. The inside of the bill is also red but the bill itself is black. In winter plumage it looks totally different. After the moult it becomes ghostly white, finely marked with black.

Puffin
Fratercula arctica
Puifin

win.   sum.

The Puffin is perhaps the best-known auk. Its dumpy upright stance, black-and-white plumage and remarkable multi-coloured bill have brought it to the attention of many. It is noticeably smaller than either the Razorbill or the Guillemot and is more stocky in appearance. Besides being coloured with red, blue, white and yellow, the bill is very deep and parrot-like. The winter plumage is much duller. Puffins also nest colonially, but in burrows in the turf at the cliff top rather than on the cliff face itself.

PIGEONS AND DOVES

Rock Dove
Columba livia
Colm aille

The Rock Dove is smaller than the Woodpigeon and lacks the white markings on the neck and wings but there is an obvious white rump patch visible in flight. Two black bars show on the wings both on the ground and in the air and there are glossy green and purple sheens on the head and breast. In the wild form, Rock Doves are found along Ireland's rocky coasts. The "feral" or street Pigeon, so familiar in Irish towns and cities, is descended from Rock Doves that have escaped or have been released from captivity.

Stock Dove
Columba oenas
Colm gorm

The Stock Dove favours agricultural land. It is similar in appearance to the Rock
Dove, though slightly smaller and neater. In flight the upperparts show none of
the striking white markings of the Rock Dove or the Woodpigeon, though there
is a dark trailing edge on the wings and tail. The head and breast have glossy
sheens like those of the Rock Dove. Although less approachable than the other
Pigeons, Stock Doves often accompany Woodpigeons feeding in the fields.

Woodpigeon
Columba palumbus
Colm coile

The Woodpigeon is the largest, most common and widespread of Ireland's pigeons. They roost in woods and large flocks feed together on seeds along roadsides, in fields, etc. The Woodpigeon has a strange gliding nuptial flight and often makes loud smacking noises with the wings. The plumage is greyish with a pink tinge on the breast and greenish tinge on the neck. There is a large white neck marking and clear white patches on the wings. The tail, which has a dark terminal band, is often fanned out in flight. As with the other Pigeons, the feet are pinkish.

Collared Dove
Streptopelia decaocto
Fearán baicdhubh

Since its first appearance in 1959, the Collared Dove has become a widespread and common resident. It is found in a wide variety of habitats but it is usually near human habitations. Although it is smaller in body than the other members of the family it has a longer tail than the others. The overall plumage is pale sandy and there are whitish sides to the tail. The undertail region is strikingly black and white, visible in flight. There is a fine black half-collar on the neck from which the name is derived.

SMALL GROUND BIRDS

Skylark
Alauda arvensis
Fuiseog stairiceach

The Skylark is Ireland's only widespread and common lark. It is well known for its remarkable display song in which it ascends vertically into the sky, singing all the while. Larger and more robust than the pipits, it is nevertheless similarly marked with heavily streaked brownish plumage and white outer tail feathers. Skylarks feed on both insects and seeds and gather in flocks in stubble fields in the winter.

Meadow Pipit
Anthus pratensis
Riabhóg mhóna

The Meadow Pipit is a common and widespread ground bird, somewhat like the Skylark, with brownish, heavily streaked plumage and white outer tail feathers. It is, however, a more delicate bird, with thinner bill, and lacks the crest on the head. Meadow Pipits call with a distinctive squeak, a very familiar open-country call.

Rock Pipit
Anthus spinoletta
Riabhóg chladaigh

The Rock Pipit is an exclusively coastal relative of the Meadow Pipit. It is larger, darker and less noticeably streaked. The outer tail feathers are paler than the others but not white. The bill and legs are blackish, not pinkish as in the Meadow Pipit. The call, too, is a bolder squeak than that of the smaller bird.

Grey Wagtail
Motacilla cinerea
Glasóg liath

The Grey Wagtail is a bird of watery habitats, particularly running streams and rivers. The back is blue-grey, the wings and tail blackish, the latter with white outer feathers. There are clear black-and-white head markings – more noticeable in the male. The underparts are lemon-yellow, deeper under the tail. In winter the summer finery of the male is dulled and both sexes are alike. The call note has a metallic, ringing quality.

Pied Wagtail
Motacilla alba
Glasóg shráide

ad.

juv.

The Pied Wagtail is a widespread species as much at home in the country as it is in the town. It is distinctively patterned with a noticeably long black-and-white tail which is constantly wagged up and down. The female is greyish on the back and the juvenile is dull and less clearly marked. The call is a clear "chissick".

SWALLOW-TYPE BIRDS

Swallow
Hirundo rustica
Fáinleog

The Swallow is a familiar and widespread summer visitor. It is glossy blue-black on the upperparts, creamy on the underparts with brick-red head patches. There is a row of white spots on the tail which become obvious when the tail is opened and closed. This is deeply forked with very long outer streamers in the adult but not in the young bird. The flock calls with pleasant twittering.

House Martin
Delichon urbica
Gabhlán binne

The House Martin is similar to the Swallow in its glossy black upperparts. The underparts and a neat rump patch are white, however. The notched tail lacks the Swallow's long streamers. The call is a tuneless "tirrup" – quite different from that of the Swallow. House Martins land on the ground during the breeding season and may be seen collecting mud to construct their unique cup-shaped nests.

Sand Martin
Riparia riparia
Gabhlán gainimh

The Sand Martin is slightly smaller than the House Martin and is warm brown above and white below with a distinct brown breast band. The tail is only slightly forked. The call is similar to that of the House Martin but is quieter. Like the House Martin, this species nests colonially but in holes in banks rather than on buildings. They arrive in Ireland in spring before the other members of the family – often before the end of March.

Swift
Apus apus
Gabhlán gaoithe

The Swift is often taken for a member of the Swallow family but in fact is only a rather distant relative. It is a longer bird, with longer narrower wings and notched tail. Although it is dark brown, the Swift normally appears black. Swifts are so totally designed for life on the wing that they can even roost in the air. The call is a high-pitched rasping or screaming. They arrive later and leave earlier than the others in this group.

SMALL BROWN BIRDS

Spotted Flycatcher
Muscicapa striata
Cuilire liath

The Spotted Flycatcher is a summer visitor to Ireland from African winter grounds but it is rather locally distributed. Insects are caught from a branch or other vantage perch, the Flycatcher flying out quickly and returning to the perch again with the prey. The plumage is grey-brown above, white below with faint marking on the brownish breast. The call is a clear "tick" and is heard frequently when the young are about.

Treecreeper
Certhia familiaris
Snag

The Treecreeper is often misnamed "woodpecker" in Ireland due to its manner of feeding – by climbing up the trunks of trees in search of insects in the bark. It is a small, delicate bird with thin curved bill designed more for probing than "pecking". The longish tail feathers are stiff and prop the bird against the tree as it climbs. The plumage is streaked brownish above and whitish below. It has a mouse-like appearance as it moves jerkily up and around a tree. The call is a thin and indistinct squeak.

Dunnock
Prunella modularis
Donnóg

The Dunnock, commonly misnamed the Hedge Sparrow (for it is not a sparrow), is a secretive and inconspicuous little bird. It is aptly named dun-ock or og (meaning "little dark one") as it is dark brown, streaked darker on the back and tinged with grey on the head and underparts. The call is a monotonous "jeep" and the song is an undistinguished little refrain.

Wren
Troglodytes troglodytes
Dreolín

The tiny Wren is one of Ireland's most familiar and certainly one of its commonest and most widespread birds. This energetic little bird with typical cocked-up tail and low buzzing flight needs little description. The plumage is heavily barred on the sides and tail and there is a warm, rusty tinge on the rump and tail. The song is incredibly loud for such a small bird and the call is a sharp "chick".

THRUSHES

Song Thrush
Turdus philomelos
Smólach

The Song Thrush is perhaps Ireland's tiniest song bird. Its plumage is warm brown above, pale below, heavily speckled with black. The spots run into one another in dark blotches and streaks. The underwings are noticeably honey-coloured sometimes visible in flight, and the call is a distinct "tsip". Song Thrushes a familiar garden birds, feeding on worms and grubs and using favoured stones "anvils" for breaking open snails.

Redwing
Turdus iliacus
Deargán sneachta

he Redwing is the northern counterpart of the Song Thrush. The brown
pperparts are darker and less warm in tone. The pale underparts are much more
eavily streaked and marked with black. There is a clear yellowish eyestripe. A
eep rusty patch is visible on the flanks and is further revealed as an underwing
tch by the Redwing in flight. The call is a thin "ts-eer". They are abundant and
despread winter visitors, mainly from Iceland.

Mistle Thrush
Turdus viscivorus
Liatráisc

The Mistle Thrush, so named for its liking of mistletoe berries, is larger than the Song Thrush and generally greyer and paler. It is spotted with black on the underparts, the spots being more distinct and less suffused. The tail is also longer and has pale tips to the outer feathers, noticeable in flight, as are the shining white underwings. The call is a harsh rattling but the song is melodious and fluty.

Fieldfare
Turdus pilaris
Sacán

The Fieldfare is about the size of the Mistle Thrush and is similarly proportioned. It is, however, a darker bird on the back, wings and tail. The head and rump are noticeably grey. The underparts are tinged yellowish, heavily speckled and blotched with black. In flight the underwings are shining white like those of the Mistle Thrush. The flight call is a distinctive "chack, chack". Large flocks are found in stubbles and other fields during the winter. Fieldfares are abundant and widespread winter visitors from Scandinavia.

GARDEN AND RIVER BIRDS

Blackbird
Turdus merula
Lon dubh

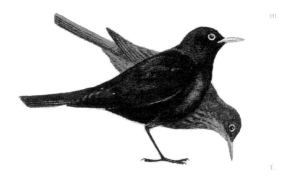

The male Blackbird's matt-black plumage and striking orange-yellow bill are so distinctive that it requires no further description. The brownish female is sometimes mistaken for a Thrush because of its pale and speckled throat but the differences are obvious from close range. The male Blackbird is one of Ireland's best song birds. Its song is deeper, with less repetition, than that of the Song Thrush, but is nonetheless similar. The alarm call is an excited squawk.

Starling
Sturnus vulgaris
Druid

ad.

juv.

The Starling is as much at home in close proximity to man as it is in open countryside, and its adaptability to circumstances is one of its outstanding characteristics. Starlings have a wide variety of call notes and as great mimics they often impersonate both natural and man-made sounds. The plumage is glossy black with fine pale speckling in summer. In winter it is more heavily specked and the young bird is brown rather than shiny black.

Dipper
Cinclus cinclus
Gabha dubh

The Dipper is about the size of a Starling but "dumpier" in shape. The dark
brown and blackish plumage is relieved only by the white throat and breast patch.
A rusty band borders the white patch but is by no means easy to see in the field.
It is named for its curious and nervous dipping as it stands on a stone in flowing
water. The call, which is often uttered as the bird flies with whirring wings close
to the water surface, is a ringing "zit". The young bird is dull greyish and lacks
the adult's white bib.

Kingfisher
Alcedo atthis
Cruidín

The Kingfisher is even smaller than the Dipper but has the plumage of an
scaped exotic bird. There are various shades of green and blue on the upperparts.
The underparts are orange and there are white and orange patches on the head.
The bill is long and heavy for the size of the bird and the small feet are bright
ed. In flight, which is rapid and direct, the Kingfisher looks like an electric blue
ash due to the bright turquoise feathers on the back and rump.

SMALL 'PERKY' BIRDS

Robin
Erithacus rubecula
Spideog

juv.

ad.

The Robin is a most familiar garden bird. It needs little description, for its warm
brown upperparts and orange-red face and breast are well known. The young
bird can be confusing, as it lacks the red breast and is heavily marked with pale
speckles. Robins are gardeners' constant companions, sometimes hopping about
within arm's reach looking for grubs and insects as they are uncovered. The call
is a pronounced "tick" and the song, which may be sung at any time of the year
by the highly territorial male, is a recognizable and pleasant warbling.

Stonechat
Saxicola torquata
Caislín cloch

The Stonechat is an ostentatious little bird which is often to be seen perched on a post or wire fence, or on a sprig of gorse, and particularly in rough ground near the sea. The Stonechat characteristically flicks its wings and tail and calls with short "chipping" notes, from which the name is derived. The male in summer is a bright little bird with black head, wings and tail and white markings on the wings and rump. The breast is orange. In winter the plumage is duller and the female looks duller throughout the year.

Wheatear
Oenanthe oenanthe
Clochrán

The Wheatear prefers to perch on walls and fences rather than on bushes. It is a summer visitor to Ireland from wintering quarters in Africa and is to be found most commonly at the coast in spring and autumn. The bird itself is at once recognizable by its white rump and black-tipped tail – a striking feature in flight. The wings are blackish and there is a black mark on the cheeks of the male. The male's upperparts are light grey and the whitish underparts are tinged yellowish on the breast. In autumn the plumage is duller, more closely resembling the brown-beaked females and juveniles. The call is a sharp "chack" and the song is a pleasant jangling.

WARBLER TYPES

Willow Warbler
Phylloscopus trochilus
Ceolaire sailí

The Willow Warbler is a common
and widespread summer visitor to
Ireland. It is found mainly in scrubby
habitats but on migration it can be
found in all kinds of cover. It is
an inconspicuous little greenish
bird, paler below and with a
yellowish tinge on the breast
of the young bird. The call is a
distinctive "lui" and the song is
a pleasant cascading warble.

Chiffchaff
Phylloscopus collybita
Tuif-teaf

The Chiffchaff is, like the Willow
Warbler, a widespread summer
visitor. Very like the Willow
Warbler, it does, however, tend
to be tinged more brown and
less yellow. Other differences,
like blackish rather than
pinkish legs, are less reliable
identifiers. The call is similar
but the song is completely
different. The name is derived
from the unmistakable "chiff-chaff",
sung from the treetops in summer.

Goldcrest
Regulus regulus
Cíorbhuí

The Goldcrest is closely
related to the warblers and
is Ireland's smallest bird. The
plumage is greenish and
whitish beneath and there are
black and white marks on the
wings. Both sexes show a flash
of colour on the top of the head
– orange in the male, yellow in
the female. The call is a thin mouse-
like squeak and the song is simply an
extended version of the same.

Sedge Warbler
Acrocephalus schoenobaenus
Ceolaire cíbe

The Sedge Warbler is a common and
widespread summer visitor to Ireland,
favouring marshy vegetation. The
upperparts are heavily streaked, there
is a distinct pale eyestripe and a rusty
tinge on the rump. The call is a harsh
single note and the song is a loud, varied
warbling with harsh sequences.

Whitethroat
Sylvia communis
Gilphib

f.   m.

The Whitethroat is a widespread summer visitor, but is nowhere particularly common. Its preferred habitat in Ireland is amongst gorse, brambles or similar vegetation in rough ground situations. The song is a jumbled chattering and the usual call is a low "churr". The male is grey on the head and white on the throat – the underparts are tinged pinkish and the back is tinged brown, rusty on the wings. The female is less colourful.

TITS

Long-tailed Tit
Aegithalos caudatus
Meantán earrfhada

The Long-Tailed Tit is the smallest o
body but has the longest tail. It differ
colour, being mainly pinkish and blac
above, greyish white below. There
are distinctive double blackish
head stripes. The main habitat
is scrubland and woods in
general. It is less a garden
bird than the others of the
family. Long-tailed Tits
feed in nomadic groups on
a wide variety of insects
and often join other small
birds in the winter. The calls
are varied and are
reminiscent of those of
the Treecreeper.

Coal Tit
Parus ater
Meantán dubh

The Coal Tit is similar in size and shape
to the Blue Tit but is quite different in
appearance. The plumage is mainly
grey and brown rather than blue and
green, and the head is black with
whitish cheeks and nape patch. The
Coal Tit calls with a whistled "tui"
and a variety of other short notes.
It is one of the commonest birds of
Ireland's conifer plantations, where it
feeds on insect life in the canopy.

Blue Tit
Parus caeruleus
Meantán gorm

The Blue Tit is the familiar "blue-bonnet" of the garden which feeds acrobatically on suspended food. It will feed on a wide variety of food, from insects to nuts. The Blue Tit is very small and compact and has a clearly marked head, yellowish underparts and green and bluish upperparts. The call is nasal and buzzing, quite different in quality from the others in the family.

Great Tit
Parus major
Meantán mór

The Great Tit is the largest of the family – roughly sparrow-sized. Like the Coal Tit, it has a black head with bright white cheeks but lacks the white nape patch. Like the Blue Tit, it is green and blue above and yellow below but there is a thick black band running from the chin to beneath the tail. In general it is a striking and beautiful bird. The calls are similar to those of the Coal Tit but the "seek-er, seek-er" song is unmistakable. It joins other small birds in winter foraging flocks.

FAMILIAR CROWS

Magpie
Pica pica
Snag breac

The Magpie must be one of Ireland's best-known birds, due largely to its pied plumage. A clever opportunist, it has learned to exploit food sources of all kinds, including the eggs and chicks of other birds. The Magpie's striking appearance and its legendary thieving habits have endeared the bird to many. The black tail and wing feathers have a green and blue sheen respectively.

Jackdaw
Corvus monedula
Cág

The Jackdaw is Ireland's smallest crow. It is well known for its rather mischievous appearance and sinister white eye. It is mainly sooty black, though the sides of the head are greyish. The Jackdaw struts rather than walks, and the call is a resonant "chack". Like the Starling, the Jackdaw has "streetwise" habits and coexists comfortably with man.

Rook
Corvus frugilegus
Rúcach

ad.

juv.

The Rook is a large crow with a more agreeable personality than some of the others. It feeds in the fields but is not above foraging on the shore or feeding on carrion at the roadside. It is very recognizable in breeding season, with its pale featherless patch at the base of the bill and rather shaggy black plumage. The young bird lacks the bare face patch and can look like an all-black Hooded Crow. Rooks call with a monotonous cawing, making the rookery a noisy and raucous woodland.

Hooded Crow
Corvus corone
Feannóg

The Hooded Crow is less associated with man than the others of this group. Although it does take eggs and young birds it does a valuable job in cleaning up carrion from the roadsides and elsewhere throughout the countryside. The Hooded Crow is so-called because of its clearly demarcated black head. The wings and tail are also black but the body is grey. The call is a rather drawn-out "gw-a-ak".

LESS FAMILIAR CROWS

Raven
Corvus corax
Fiach dubh

The Raven is a massive bird, being substantially larger and heavier than the Rook or the Hooded Crow. On the ground the most obvious features are the outsize, powerful-looking bill and the shaggy-looking throat. In the air Ravens have longer wings and tails than the other crows, the wings showing "fingered" ends and the tail being quite diamond-shaped. During the breeding season Ravens perform spectacular rolling and tumbling exercises in flight and call with a variety of strange notes near the nest site. The usual call is a resonant "pruck' or similar croak.

Jay
Garrulus glandar
Scréachóg

The Jay is about the size of a Jackdaw but much more attractively coloured.
Brownish pink is the general colour but there are black-and-white patches
on the wings, and the tail and rump are respectively blackish and white. A
"kingfisher-blue" patch is evident at the bend of the wing and there is a black
mark on the face at the base of the bill. Jays are excitable birds and when uttering
their squawking calls they raise and lower a rough crest on the top of the head.
They rarely afford a good view and are most usually seen flying in or around
  wood.

Chough
Pyrrhocorax pyrrhocorax
Cág cosdearg

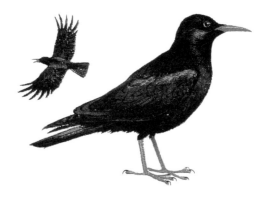

The Chough could be regarded as one of Ireland's speciality birds, as it is more abundant and widespread here than elsewhere in western Europe. It is nevertheless restricted to wilder coastal areas, especially in the west. It is slightly larger than the Jackdaw, more elegant in shape and with glossier black plumage. The bill and legs are bright red, the former with a slight downward curve. In flight the Chough has broad "finger-ended" wings and, like the Raven, performs marvellous tumbling aerobatics during the breeding season. The name "chough" (as in "rough") is derived from the wild and evocative call "keeow" which has a far-carrying quality.

FINCHES

Chaffinch
Fringilla coelebs
Rí rua

m.

f.

he Chaffinch is a familiar garden bird. The white wing and outer tail markings
e features of both sexes, particularly in flight. On the ground the male can be
en to be an attractively coloured finch with blue cap, green and brown on the
ck and with brick-coloured cheeks and underparts. The female is duller. The
ll is a distinctive "pink" and the song is a pleasant jangling.

Greenfinch
Carduelis chloris
Glasán darach

The Greenfinch is even stockier than the Bullfinch, with a very stout pinkish bill which will deal with almost any kind of seed. Both sexes are alike in having greenish plumage and bright yellow flashes on the wings and at the sides of the tail. The young birds have duller plumage, but have the stout beak and general appearance of the adults.

Goldfinch
Carduelis carduelis
Lasair choille

The Goldfinch is a most attractive finch with its black, white and sandy plumage, red face and bright yellow wing flashes. The beautiful plumage of both sexes and the pleasant liquid notes of the song are well known. It is more of an open country bird than the other finches, and will feed avidly on the seeds of thistles and other weeds.

Siskin
Carduelis spinus
Siscín

m.

f.

The Siskin is somewhat like a miniature Greenfinch, being predominantly greenish, but it is more tit-like in behaviour. The male is clearly marked, with black on the chin, top of the head and streaks on the back. There are yellow flashes on the wings and tail. The female is a duller version of the male. Siskins call with lively twitterings as they move from treetop to treetop, feeding on the cones of a variety of trees.

Bullfinch
Pyrrhula pyrrhula
Corcrán coille

m.

f.

The male Bullfinch is blue-grey above, soft pink below and on the cheeks. There is a black cap on the head and the wings and tail are also black. The female's plumage is much duller but both sexes show a clear white wing bar and rump in flight. Bullfinches call with a soft "beoo". With their stout bill they are well equipped to deal with seeds of all kinds.

FINCH-TYPE BIRDS

House Sparrow
Passer domesticus
Gealbhan binne

The House Sparrow is
familiar to everyone. So well
does it coexist with man that
it is rarely to be found far
from buildings. Sparrows
have seed-eating bills like
the finches but will eat
almost any household
scrap. The male is quite
well marked, with grey
and rust-brown head,
brown back and
black throat. The female
is a rather nondescript
grey-brown.

Linnet
Carduelis cannabina
Gleoiseach

The Linnet is a little finch associated
most commonly with rough and
uncultivated ground. At the
breeding site the male sings with
an extended and pleasant song.
The male in breeding plumage
has a red smudge on the breast
and forehead; the remainder of
the head is greyish and the back
is brown. The female is duller. In
winter, males and females are alike
but both show distinctive pale flashes
on the edges of the wings and tail.

Redpoll
Carduelis flammea
Deargéadan

The Redpoll is rather like a small, slim
Linnet. In breeding plumage the male has
reddish markings on the head and breast.
The female is duller, more obviously
streaked, and lacks the red smudge on the
breast. Both have a black chin mark and
clear pale wing bars. Redpolls are highly
active feeders. The flock calls with a variety of
twittering notes, including a buzzing trill. They
are recognizable, even at a distance, by their
tiny size and cleft tail.

Yellowhammer
Emberiza citrinella
Buíóg

The Yellowhammer is a most
attractive member of this
family. It is a slim bird with
yellow head and breast and
red-brown, heavily streaked
back. The rump is particularly
rust-coloured and noticeable
in flight, as are the white
outer feathers. The female
is a duller version of the
male. The usual call is a
loud "chick" and the song
sounds like "a little bit of
bread and no ch-e-e-e-se".
The main habitats are gorse-
covered commonages and
some hedgerows.

m.

f.

Reed Bunting
Emberiza schoeniclus
Gealóg ghiolcaí

The Reed Bunting is
similar in size to the
Yellowhammer, with
streaked back and white
outer tail feathers, but the
male has a black head
and throat and whitish
underparts. The female
is quite different, being
generally brown, but
is richly streaked with
black. The call is a thin
"tiu" and the song is
an unremarkable little
jangling. The main habitat
is in reedbeds or marshy
ground but it is also found in scrub,
sometimes well away from water.

m.

f.

INDEX